D0394891

CHRISTOPHER COLUMBUS

Peter and Connie Roop

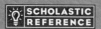

For all of the young authors at Highlands Elementary School in Appleton, Wisconsin.
May your voyages with words carry you to faraway lands.

ACKNOWLEDGMENTS
Thomas C. Tirado, Ph.D., History Department, Millersville University, for reviewing the manuscript and making insightful suggestions.
Chief Torres of the Jatibonicù Band of the Taíno tribe for his input into the book and his comments regarding Native Americans.
Castello Banfi for his gastronomic ideas and knowledge of the foods of the fifteenth century.
The Milwaukee Public Museum for its ongoing displays of Native American life.
The Smithsonian Institution for its remarkable "Seeds of Change" exhibit.
The Tourist Board of Santo Domingo for their materials relating to their wonderful island and its native peoples.

Library of Congress Cataloging-in-Publication Data
Roop, Connie.
Christopher Columbus / by Connie Roop and Peter Roop.
p. cm. — (In their own words)
Includes biographical references and index.
Summary: Recounts the life story of the noted explorer, including excerpts from his own writings.
1. Columbus, Christopher—Juvenile Literature. 2. Explorers—America—Biography—Juvenile Literature. 3. Explorers—Spain—Biography—Juvenile literature. 4. America—Discovery and exploration—Spanish—Juvenile literature [1. Columbus, Christopher. 2. Explorers. 3. America—Discovery and exploration—Spanish.] I. Roop, Peter. II. Title. III. In their own words (Scholastic)
E111.R78 2000 • 970.01'5'092—dc21 • [B]   99-088546
ISBN 0-439-27180-0 (pob) • ISBN 0-439-15807-9 (pb)

10 9 8 7 6 5 4 3   02 03 04 05

Composition by Brad Walrod
Printed in the U.S.A.   23
First trade printing, September 2001

CONTENTS

INTRODUCTION

"I THOUGHT OF WRITING ON THIS WHOLE voyage, very diligently, all that I would do and see and experience." Christopher Columbus wrote these words in his *diario*, his journal. They describe his first voyage across the unknown Atlantic Ocean. He brought this first journal to Queen Isabella and King Ferdinand of Spain upon his return from the New World in 1493.

Columbus kept a journal on each of his four voyages to the Americas. In them he recorded the wind, weather, people, and places he encountered. He told of his landfall on October 12, 1492, in what he thought were the Indies. He described his hunt for gold and the capture of

"Indians." He wrote about being placed in chains during his third voyage. He expressed excitement about seeing a new continent for the first time.

Columbus returned to Europe from his first voyage in March 1493. He was very eager to share his adventures with the queen and king who had paid for his voyage. But he had to travel many days to reach the royal court. To prepare Isabella and Ferdinand he wrote a letter telling of his amazing success. Later, he would bring his *diario* to them. Sadly, this journal, as well as a copy of it ordered by Isabella, was eventually lost. To this day, no one knows where they are.

How do we know what Columbus thought in 1492 when he began his adventure? What did he experience as he traveled across the Atlantic in search of the fabled Indies? How did he feel when he reached land at last? Fortunately, Bartolomé de Las Casas, who sailed with Columbus on his third voyage, copied much of the original *diario* before it disappeared.

By reading the journal Las Casas copied, you hear

Columbus's writings, such as letters like this one, help us understand what he saw and experienced.

what Columbus thought, felt, and experienced. Reading Columbus's *diario* you feel as though you are standing beside Columbus on the *Santa María*. You smell the salty wind in your face. You gaze across the mysterious western sea. You feel Columbus's determination to find a water route to the rich Indies. You hear the fearful crew grumble. You can even sense Columbus's frustration as his men almost force him to abandon his dream.

You delight in seeing "very green trees and many ponds and fruits of various kind" after thirty-three days at sea. You thrill as Columbus steps ashore in a world that was new to him.

But for the Native Americans living on the island "called Guanahani in the language of the Indians," this world was not new. It was their world. Columbus was new to it. Yet it is through his eyes that Europeans saw this world for the first time.

Writing his *diario* was a challenge for Columbus. He wrote in Spanish. Each day he had to write the distance his three ships traveled. He had to record the wind and weather. He wrote with quill pens fashioned from feathers. His quill pens needed constant sharpening. Every two or three words he had to dip his pen into his ink. He had to write quickly before the ink dried. And he had to write no matter how much the *Santa María* rolled on rough seas.

No one is sure what Christopher Columbus looked like because no paintings exist of him from his lifetime. These paintings are based on written descriptions of Columbus.

What Columbus wrote helps us understand his voyages and his life. We call his *diario* a primary source. Primary sources are the real accounts of a person's experiences. They are records of events a person saw or experienced. Letters, diaries, and journals are primary sources. Reading a primary source is like talking with someone from the past.

The journals of Lewis and Clark, for example, are

a primary source. The Declaration of Independence is a primary source. A photograph you take at a party is a primary source. If you keep a journal, it is a primary source, too.

We also learn from secondary sources. These are descriptions of events written by someone who was not there. Ferdinand Columbus's biography of his father is a secondary source. The entries in an encyclopedia are secondary sources. This book is a secondary source although it contains some writing from primary sources.

In this book we use Columbus's *diario* as our primary sources. We use many other books as secondary sources. A primary source is the next best thing to being there. Through the writer's words you feel the joy of discovery. You dread the terror of a storm at sea. You gaze in wonder at sights not seen before. You hear of his or her worries, fears, joys, and triumphs.

WEST TO THE INDIES

"WE DEPARTED THE THIRD DAY OF August of the year 1492 from the [sand] bar of Saltés [a river in Spain] at the eighth hour." What a thrill it must have been for Christopher Columbus to write those words! For years the tall, red-haired captain had dreamed of sailing west to the rich Indies. At forty-one years old, he was setting out on a remarkable adventure, a dream come true. Standing on the deck of the *Santa María*, Columbus watched with pride as his companion ships, the *Niña* and the *Pinta*, followed along behind him. The voyage into the unknown had finally begun.

No one knows when Columbus first got the idea to sail west across the Atlantic to reach the riches of the Indies. But for years he battled hardship and disappointment to reach his goal.

For centuries sailors and scholars knew the earth was round, like a ball. After all, the mast top was the first part of a ship seen over the horizon. For this to happen the earth had to be round. Also, Columbus thought that the ocean on the European shore was the same ocean that touched the Indies. Believing all this, Columbus thought he could reach the Indies by sailing west.

Christopher Columbus trusted that he and his men could do what no European had ever done before. They would reach the Indies by sailing west. They would return with their ships' holds brimming with gold, silks, jewels, and spices.

The people of Europe had long enjoyed the riches of the Indies. Silks and spices had reached Europe for hundreds of years. But none had come directly by sea. The continent of Africa blocked the way. No one was able to sail around its southern tip until 1488.

Instead, the riches of the East had to be carried on camels, donkeys, and horses across Asia. Warring tribes raided the caravans. Dangerous thieves stole valuable goods. What survived then had to be transported across the Mediterranean Sea. These ships had to avoid plundering pirates and fierce storms.

Still, Europeans hungered for the spices, gold, silks, and silver of the East. They were willing to pay well for these luxuries. Venice and Genoa, two Italian cities, controlled this trade in Europe. Venice and Genoa were rich, powerful cities. They did not want other European countries

European explorers hoped to reach the riches of the Indies by sailing around Africa.

to find another way to the Indies. Jealous kings and queens of other countries, however, wished to do so.

Great riches would come to the person who discovered a faster, safer route. Great wealth would also come to the country of such an explorer. Columbus was determined to be that explorer.

In 1492, when Columbus sailed, few people believed the earth was flat. As early as 500 B.C., the scholar Pythagoras had suggested the earth was round. Fifteen hundred years before Columbus sailed, the geographer Strabo said, "If the Atlantic Ocean were not so extremely large, we could sail from [Spain] to India." Strabo even suggested that a new continent lay to the west of Europe.

One major problem, however, was distance. Just how far west would a ship have to sail to reach the Indies? Columbus and others calculated and recalculated. Columbus argued with scholars who disagreed with his calculations. He believed the ocean was only 2,500 miles (4,023 kilometers) across. With favorable winds, he could sail that in a month.

Bartolomé de Las Casas, who met Columbus (above) in 1500, described him as a man "of lofty thoughts."

Columbus was wrong. His figures were off by thousands of miles. He thought the earth was much smaller than its actual size. Columbus would have to sail over 20,000 miles (32,187 kilometers) to reach Japan. But in 1492, Columbus did not know that. He believed his three ships could sail to the Indies and back. For years this belief powered his dream.

But Columbus had to convince someone to sponsor him. He did not have the money to outfit ships himself. He needed a king or a queen to help him. In 1484, he tried King John II of Portugal. The king turned him down. In 1485, he begged Queen Isabella of Spain. No, she told him. In 1490, he sent his brother to the king of France. Again, no was the answer.

Columbus was not a man to give up. He persisted until Isabella at last agreed to help him. By 1492, she, too, wanted the wealth of the Indies. She agreed to help Columbus.

In his *diario* Columbus explained what the king and queen wanted him to do on his voyage. He wrote, "You [Queen Isabella and King Ferdinand] commanded that I should not go to the East by land, by which it is customary to go, but by the route to the West, by which route we do not know for certain that anyone previously has passed." This route to the west meant leaving the sight of land. It meant sailing across the vast and uncharted Atlantic Ocean. No one knew how long such a voyage might take. No one knew if such a voyage was even possible.

When the *Santa María*, *Pinta*, and *Niña* set sail Columbus had another goal in mind. He desired to bring Christianity to the peoples of the Indies. A devout Catholic, he wished to convert all he met to his religion.

"You [Isabella and Ferdinand] thought of sending me, Christopher Columbus, to the [Indies] to see the princes and the peoples and the lands and the characteristics of the lands and of everything, and to see how their conversion to our Holy Faith might be undertaken."

So it was on August 3, 1492, that Columbus and ninety other men left Europe to sail into history.

BOYHOOD IN GENOA

WHO WAS COLUMBUS? WHY WAS he determined to reach the Indies? Perhaps the answer lies in his childhood.

Christopher Columbus was born in Genoa within sight of the sea. His actual birthday is unknown. Most scholars think he was born sometime between August and October 1451. In 1502, Columbus wrote in a letter, "In the city of Genoa I have my roots, and there I was born." It was in an ancient church in Genoa that he was baptized and given his Italian name, Cristoforo Colombo. In English, he is Christopher Columbus.

Christopher Columbus was loyal to his native Genoa throughout his life. He never became a citizen of anyplace else.

During Columbus's childhood, Genoa was a busy port. Ships from across the Mediterranean Sea landed there. They unloaded cargoes of pepper, silk, tea, and spices. Wool, copper, lead, tin, and weapons were then loaded to be sent east. Ships were built in Genoa. Mapmakers made their homes there. One explorer from Genoa even tried to sail around Africa in 1291. Another discovered the Canary Islands far out in the Atlantic.

As a boy, Columbus would have watched these ships enter and leave the port. He would have listened to sailors' thrilling stories of strange lands. He would have heard the marvelous tales from Marco Polo's book *Description of the World*. Polo's book was the most famous book about the Indies. Columbus certainly gazed upon the waters of the Mediterranean, wondering what lay beyond them.

Although he probably dreamed of the sea as a young man, Columbus worked in the family cloth business. His grandfathers and father were weavers. His mother wove cloth. As the oldest child of five, Columbus was also expected to become a weaver.

Columbus did not learn to read or write as a child. His parents could not afford to send him to school. He learned reading and writing later in life. But from his father he learned how to clean wool. He learned how to card (comb) wool to remove dirt and tangles. He probably wove wool into cloth with his mother and favorite brother, Bartholomew.

Young Christopher did not want to be a weaver all his life. As he wrote later, "At a very tender age

I entered upon sea sailing and so have I continued to this day." No records remain to tell us how he got his start. Maybe he sailed on trading ships carrying his father's woolen cloth. Maybe he sailed with local fishermen. Although we don't know who Columbus sailed with, we know he ventured upon the sea as a young man.

AT SEA

COLUMBUS WROTE IN HIS *DIARIO* ON December 21, 1492, "I have followed the sea for 23 years without leaving it for any time worth reckoning."

He was a long way from his boyhood home. His journey had taken many twists and turns and brought him across the Atlantic.

As an adult, Columbus knew how to make charts. He knew how to sail a ship and navigate. He could gauge distances accurately. History does not tell us how he gained these skills. No records exist describing his learning to be a seaman. Yet he did. In order to safely guide his fleet across the Atlantic in 1492, Christopher Columbus had to be a master mariner.

Hints from history have Columbus sailing as a young man on trading ships from Genoa. What he learned about sailing he did not learn from books. He learned his skills by doing them day after day, night after night.

In 1476, when he was twenty-five, Columbus took part in an adventure that helped set his course for America. Tradition holds that he sailed from Genoa with a fleet of ships that held valuable cargo. To protect the cargo, a warship sailed along with the fleet.

This was Columbus's first voyage on the Atlantic. It ended in disaster. Along the southern coast of Portugal, enemy ships attacked. The battle raged all day. By night, seven ships sank and hundreds of sailors drowned.

The *Bechella*, upon which Columbus sailed, was one of those which sank. During the battle, Columbus was wounded. As the ship sank, Columbus jumped overboard and grabbed a large floating oar. Clinging to it for life, he swam over six miles (10 kilometers) to shore. He landed near

Lagos, Portugal. There he found safety and comfort until his wound healed. Then he walked many miles to Lisbon, the capital of Portugal.

Lisbon, in 1476, was an important European city. Ships sailed from its port to Africa, Iceland, England, and dozens of Mediterranean seaports.

Portugal's Prince Henry the Navigator created a navigation school at the seaport of St. Vincent's. Although not a sailor himself (for royalty did not sail ships), Prince Henry wished to discover more about the unknown oceans. He wanted to sail his ships around the tip of Africa.

To find a new way to the Indies, Prince Henry planned and paid for more than fifty journeys along the African coast.

Prince Henry's ships carefully explored down Africa's northwest coast. They did not reach Cape Horn, Africa's southern tip. The ships failed to round

Cape Bojador, Africa's western bulge. Each captain returned with tales of terror about what lay south of Cape Bojador. But they also returned with African pepper, gold, ivory, and slaves.

Henry sent his ships to explore the Atlantic, too. Portugal claimed the islands of the Azores, Cape Verde, and Madeira. His people settled them and began a profitable trade. And the captains of Henry's vessels returned with a wealth of information.

Much of the information was put on maps. When Columbus landed in Portugal, Lisbon had the best mapmakers in the world. Arriving in Lisbon, Columbus was penniless. He did not know how to speak Portuguese.

Then Columbus's luck suddenly changed. Who should be making maps in Lisbon? None other than his favorite brother, Bartholomew! Christopher joined Bartholomew in the mapmaking business. Here he would gain more of the skills needed for his great adventures.

They took new information from sea captains. They added this information to old maps to update them. History leaves us few other details about the Columbus brothers in Portugal. A terrible earthquake and fire in 1755 destroyed much of Lisbon and its written records.

But Columbus did not want to make maps forever. He wanted to add to the maps himself. So he went to sea again. This time he sailed north to Holland, England, Ireland, and even Iceland.

During his travels he heard stories of lands to the west. The Viking explorer Erik the Red had settled in Greenland. His son Leif the Lucky had even discovered a new land 500 years before. He named this place "Vinland" for the number of berries growing there. The Vikings built a colony in what is now Newfoundland, Canada. But they were forced out by angry *Skraellings*, the Viking word for Native Americans.

Surely Columbus listened to these tales and wondered what lay just west over the horizon. During his time in Portugal, Columbus mastered navigation. He improved his skills with the compass. He learned how to find latitude (a ship's

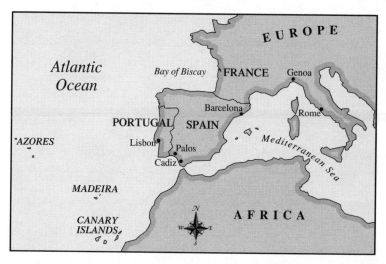

In 1476, Columbus moved to Lisbon, a city in western Portugal.

distance north or south of the equator) by the position of the stars. He became skilled at dead reckoning, estimating how far a ship sailed in a day.

And he improved his reading and writing. He made notes in the margins of his favorite books. "All seas are navigable." "Every country has its east or west." "Where the sun sets, an unknown country."

He bought Marco Polo's *The Description of the World* (Columbus's copy has been preserved for five centuries). He underlined "pearls, precious stones, brocades, ivory, pepper, nuts, nutmeg, cloves, and an

It is believed that Columbus learned Latin during his first years in Portugal. He needed to know Latin to read important books from the past.

abundance of other spices." He purchased and studied Pliny's *Natural History*.

Columbus owned *Imago Mundi* (Image of the World) as well. This book described the world, stating that the Atlantic Ocean "is not so great that it can cover three quarters of the globe." Columbus believed this, for it meant his route to the Indies would be shorter than expected. The *Imago Mundi*, well thumbed by Columbus, can still be seen in

Spain today. Its margins are filled with notes Columbus made. Columbus carried these books with him on all of his voyages. He treasured them until his death.

By 1478, Columbus was a capable mariner. A ship owner hired him. He sailed to the island of Madeira in the Atlantic to buy sugar.

The next year, Columbus married Dona Felipa Perestrello e Moniz. He was twenty-eight. She was twenty-five. They moved to an island near Madeira where Dona Felipa's brother was governor. Columbus could have easily chosen to settle down. He had married. He could live comfortably off the money he earned sailing and the money that Dona Felipa had. In 1480, his first son, Diego, was born. But he had an urge to see what lay beyond the western horizon.

One day Diego would follow his then-famous father across the Atlantic Ocean to a new world. But for now Christopher Columbus was only a man with a dream.

THE ENTERPRISE
OF THE INDIES

IN 1541, COLUMBUS'S SECOND SON, Ferdinand, wrote a biography of his father. He said, "One thing led to another and gave life to many thoughts, so that the Admiral [Columbus], while in Portugal began to think that it should be possible to sail equally far to the west, and that it was logical to find land in that direction."

While living in Portugal and sailing the Atlantic, Columbus heard many legends. One told of fabulous lands to the west. Sailors had glimpsed these enchanted places. But the lands vanished before anyone could set foot on them.

Real evidence of distant peoples and places washed ashore. He had seen pieces of strangely carved wood on the beach. Huge trunks of trees unknown in Europe had drifted in.

Columbus noted in one of his books, "Men from Cathay [China] which lies toward the east, have arrived here. We have seen many remarkable things, above all in Ireland, a man and a woman outlandish in appearance, in two drifting boats."

Columbus kept learning. He kept sailing, making trips down the coast of Africa and north to the English Channel. He worked on maps and charts and perfected his sailing skills.

Columbus studied ocean currents and winds. And he learned the skills he needed to be the captain of a ship and its crew. He wrote in his copy of the *Imago Mundi*, "Note that often when sailing from Lisbon south I made careful study of the course we followed, as pilots and mariners do." Using his instruments he calculated that "The circumference of the earth at the equator is 20,400 miles [32,831 kilometers]."

Later this proved to be a major mistake. The earth is over 25,000 miles (40,234 kilometers) around at the equator. Columbus did not know this.

Using what he did know, he set out to prove that the sea between Spain and the Indies was narrow. He calculated that only 2,400 miles (3,862 kilometers) of ocean separated Spain from the Indies. No one could convince him otherwise.

Other thinkers said the same thing. They agreed with Columbus that the Indies could be reached by sailing west. However, these men only talked. Columbus was determined to make the voyage.

In 1484, Columbus took his idea to King John II of Portugal. King John had sent his captains farther and farther down the African coast. He wished to be the first to reach the wealth of the Indies by rounding Africa by sea and crossing the Indian Ocean.

The king listened to an enthusiastic Columbus. But he turned him down. The king's advisers had argued that Japan could not be 2,400 miles (3,862 kilometers) away as Columbus proposed.

Yet King John liked Columbus. He invited Columbus to join his own explorations. But Columbus would not give up his dream.

Next Columbus turned to Spain for help. His wife,

Columbus and his son Diego walked from Palos to the Franciscan monastery of La Rábida.

Dona Felipa, had died in 1484, so he had no ties to Portugal anymore. With five-year-old Diego in tow, he went to Palos, Spain. He brought Diego to a monastery for schooling. Then Columbus approached several wealthy Spaniards for ships. They declined to participate in such a risky gamble. But one noble suggested that Queen Isabella might be interested in his venture.

Columbus presented his plans to Queen Isabella

and King Ferdinand. The queen liked the idea. However, she would let her advisers decide if she should help Columbus.

Columbus waited. And he waited. To support himself, he sold books. Meanwhile, he fell in love with Beatriz Enríquez de Harana. In 1488, their son, Ferdinand Columbus, was born.

In 1490, the queen's advisers finally gave their answer. They said no. The Atlantic could not possibly be as narrow as Columbus said. "How does he know anyway?" they asked. They told the queen it would not be wise to invest money in such an uncertain enterprise.

Columbus, not a man to give up easily, wrote to King John II of Portugal again. The king wrote saying, "We desire you to come to Us, both because you yourself have indicated such a wish, as well as other reasons; for your industry and great talent will be useful to Us." Columbus's spirits soared. King John was planning a voyage around Africa all the way to the Indies. Columbus would be part of it.

So Columbus hurried to Lisbon. There he was disappointed again. No sooner had he arrived, than the explorer Bartholomeu Dias sailed into Lisbon. He had wonderful news for the king. He had sailed around the tip of Africa. The way to the Indies was open at last! King John no longer needed Columbus's services.

Columbus refused to give up. He still believed a western sea route to the Indies would be safer and shorter than going all the way around Africa. Through his brother Bartholomew, Columbus asked King Henry VII of England for help. No was the answer. He tried King Charles VIII of France. Again, no.

But Columbus was sure of himself. He was determined to succeed. He believed he could persuade Queen Isabella. So he returned to the Spanish royal court at Granada.

The time was right. In January 1492, Queen Isabella and King Ferdinand had defeated their enemies, the Moors. The Moors had occupied parts of Spain for hundreds of years. The queen could now turn her attention to other ventures. Columbus prayed that his would be one.

Queen Isabella said no once more. Crushed,

This image shows Columbus (center) with Queen Isabella and King Ferdinand. The picture is one scene from the bronze doors at the entrance to the Rotunda in the U.S. Capitol in Washington, D.C.

Columbus left the court to get his son Diego. He rode out of town on a borrowed mule.

Then, a messenger came thundering after him. Queen Isabella and King Ferdinand had changed their minds. The monarchs would support the enterprise of the Indies after all!

THE SHIPS
AND CREWS

WHAT HAD CHANGED THE MONARCH'S minds? Partly, it was Columbus's personality. He was so eager, so sure of himself. The queen liked bold projects, such as driving the Moors from Spain. Also, Columbus had convinced Luis de Santangel of the value of his ideas. De Santangel was a powerful friend of the queen. He offered to share the risk. He would supply money himself. Queen Isabella agreed. She would put up half the money if others, including Columbus, gave the rest. Reluctantly, King Ferdinand agreed, too.

Now that Columbus had the backing of the king and queen, he made more demands. He wanted ten percent of the wealth he found. The queen and king agreed (ninety percent would remain theirs). Columbus demanded to be named Admiral of the Ocean. "Fine," said the queen (it cost her nothing). Columbus asked to be made Viceroy and Governor in command of lands discovered. "Yes," the queen consented.

In April 1492, a contract between Columbus and the queen and king was written. It stated that Columbus was "to discover and acquire with certain Vessels and people of Ours certain islands and Mainland in the Ocean Sea." It also stated that since "you [Columbus] are endangering yourself in Our Service that you will be rewarded." Columbus eagerly signed it.

Now Columbus had to find his ships and crews and sail west.

"I came to the town of Palos, which is a seaport, where I fitted out three vessels."

The vessels were the *Santa María*, the *Niña*, and the *Pinta*.

Queen Isabella ordered the people of Palos to give

Columbus's three ships set sail.

Columbus two ships for a year's voyage. She did this to punish them because they had supported her enemies. The people of Palos gave the *Niña* and the *Pinta*. The *Santa María* on which Columbus sailed was rented.

Columbus had wanted a larger ship. The *Santa María* was only about 60 feet (18 meters) long. She was slow. She was built to carry cargo. She was not built for exploration. However, the *Santa María* was the only other ship available. Columbus had to make do with her.

The Pinzón brothers of Palos joined Columbus. Martín Pinzón captained the *Pinta*. The *Pinta* was small and fast. Later, Martín Pinzón would race ahead in the *Pinta* as he tried to be the first to see land. His brother, Vicente, was captain of the *Niña*. She was the smallest of the fleet and was quick and sturdy. Over her life, the *Niña* sailed across the Atlantic with Columbus three times.

For the next three months Columbus was busy outfitting his fleet. He had his ships. Now he needed men to crew them. This was difficult. Few sailors at that time had ever sailed out of sight of land. They believed lurking sea monsters swallowed whole ships.

The men also feared that if they sailed too far west they would never return home.

Queen Isabella ordered convicted criminals to sail with Columbus. Luckily, only four men were found, for Columbus needed skilled men to sail his fleet into the unknown.

The Pinzón brothers, well respected in Palos, helped. They knew the best people for such a venture. Slowly, Columbus was able to gather his crews. He signed on sailors, servants, surgeons, carpenters, painters, and pilots. He needed caulkers to fix the ships' leaks and coopers to make barrels and casks. He needed people of many different skills for he knew not what dangers and difficulties he might encounter, and he planned to be gone for a year.

Columbus had a crew of forty on the *Santa María*. Twenty-four men and boys manned the *Niña*. The *Pinta* carried twenty-six. Almost all were Spanish. There were no women.

The three ships had open decks. Kegs, ropes, sails, food, trade goods, and supplies were stored below the deck and on deck. Only the captains had cabins. The sailors ate in the open air. They slept in whatever dry place they could find, curled on coils of rope or huddled against barrels.

Each ship had its own captain, but Columbus commanded the fleet. He set the speed of the fleet. He set the direction they would sail. Columbus made all of the major decisions.

There were no cooks on the ships. The men ate

pickled beef and pork, salted fish, biscuits, cheese, peas, garlic, onions, and beans. Fresh water was a problem. Before they left Palos, barrels of water were put aboard each ship. However, the water soon was covered with scum.

After years of praying and planning, Columbus was at last ready to sail. On August 2, the men went ashore to pray. Many wondered if they would ever see their families and friends again.

Before the sun rose on August 3, 1492, the *Santa María*, the *Niña*, and the *Pinta* raised their anchors. Columbus wrote, "I left the port, very well provided with supplies and with many seamen, on the third day of August.... I took the route to Your Highnesses' Canary Islands... in order from there to take my course and sail so far that I would reach the Indies."

As he would most days until his return, Columbus wrote in his journal. "We went south with a strong sea breeze 60 miles [97 kilometers] until sunset." The voyage had begun.

CHAPTER 7

AMERICA IN 1492

WHAT WAS AMERICA LIKE WHEN Columbus set sail? What would he find when he crossed the Ocean Sea? Columbus, of course, expected to find the Indies: China, Japan, and rich spice islands near them. He believed he would find enough gold, silk, and spices to fill his three ships.

America in 1492 was very different from Europe. Yet in many ways it was the same.

Over 100 million people lived in North and South America in 1492. Native Americans lived everywhere from the frozen ice of the Arctic to the tip of South America. They inhabited the scattered islands of the Caribbean where

This is a drawing of the ancient city of Tiahuanacu. Native Americans built large cities like this one many years before Columbus arrived.

Columbus would soon land. They had peopled the continents for at least 25,000 years.

Just like Europeans, some Native Americans lived in cities, towns, and villages.

Others lived in small family groups. They made clothes from animal skins or plants. They raised corn, potatoes, tomatoes, pumpkins, cacao beans, and peanuts (all foods unknown to Europeans). Some grew cotton. Others planted tobacco. Some hunted buffalo, bear, and deer. They fished and gathered shellfish.

Native Americans traveled by foot or canoe (horses were introduced by Columbus on his second voyage). They traded food, shells, copper, and flint. They built beautiful temples of cut stone. They worshipped. They created jewelry and art. Some studied the stars and had calendars. Others had written languages. They built homes of mud, wood, or animal skins. Some lived in buildings much like apartments. Others lived far from their neighbors.

Native Americans spoke over 2,000 different languages. They lived in many kinds of societies. They varied in looks. Some were tall. Others short. Some had sharp cheekbones. Others had round faces.

They had no metal tools. Soft copper was usually worn as jewelry. Tools were made from materials at hand: wood, bone, and stone. They had no wheels, except on children's toys.

One big difference between Europeans and Native Americans, however, was how the native peoples thought of land. They did not believe in owning land as the Europeans did. This difference would cause many problems after Columbus arrived.

Some people have called these varied peoples "Indians." Columbus was the first to call Native Americans "Indians." This is because when he met them, he thought he was in the Indies. So the people he met must have been "Indians."

Native Americans lived and died knowing nothing of Europe. Just as Columbus knew nothing of the Americas.

CHAPTER 8

THE FIRST VOYAGE

WHEN COLUMBUS AND HIS SHIPS reached the Canary Islands, the explorers bought fresh supplies. Columbus wanted enough food and water for a year's voyage.

Columbus was eager to leave. But the *Pinta* had a broken rudder and the ship could not be steered. Columbus frantically searched for a ship to replace it. One could not be found so the *Pinta* was repaired.

On September 6, 1492, the real voyage began. Columbus set his course to the west. As the Canary Islands disappeared below the horizon, the men saw their last view of anything European for seven months. The *Santa María* led the way.

The other two ships trailed in her wake. Columbus wrote, "Following the sun we left the old world."

Columbus knew his crews were fearful. He felt his men would be even more scared as they sailed farther away from Spain and land. Columbus made a plan to calm the men. He would write in two journals. In his private one he recorded the actual distance the ships had traveled. In the other, available to the pilots and crews, he reported fewer miles. Columbus did this "so in case the voyage were long the men would not be frightened and lose courage."

The sailors settled into a routine. They raised and lowered the sails. They ate and slept. They sang and told stories. They gazed at the uncharted waters ahead. They prayed. They hungered for signs of land. One day the *Niña* reported seeing a "tern and a tropic bird and these birds never depart from land more than 25 leagues [about 75 miles or 121 kilometers]." Another day they saw green plants floating on the water. They guessed these had recently been torn from land.

On September 17, Columbus wrote that "those signs were from the west where I hope in that mighty God in Whose hands are all victories that very soon He will give us land." Columbus offered a prize of his own, a silk jacket, in addition to the reward Queen Isabella promised to the first man to see land.

Columbus on board the Santa María. *He gazes out over the water and wonders what lies ahead.*

The next day, Martín Pinzón in the *Pinta* sprinted ahead. He wished to claim the prizes. Columbus was angry about this for he desired the queen's reward himself. Pinzón found no land.

The three lonely ships sailed west. One night they saw a blazing meteor, "a marvelous branch of fire fall from the sky into the sea." The superstitious sailors were scared. Was it a sign they should turn back? No, said Columbus. They sailed on. By September 20, they had traveled about 1,100 miles (1,770 kilometers).

How did Columbus know where they were? First, he had a compass. Europeans had used the compass since the twelfth century. Columbus used his compass to make certain his ships steered west.

To measure how fast they sailed Columbus used a log. Every hour the log (tied with a rope) was heaved overboard. Two marks were cut into the *Santa María*'s railing. Measuring the amount of time it took the log to pass between these marks, Columbus could tell how fast they were sailing. Each day on his map Columbus charted how far they had traveled. He entered the distance and direction in the public logbook. He also recorded them in his private journal. Columbus was a master at measuring distance. Quite possibly he was one of the best sailors ever at this skill of "dead reckoning."

When not on duty, the sailors looked for more signs of land. They saw seaweed, birds, driftwood, and towering clouds. Each sign gave hope that they would safely reach land.

On September 25, Martín Pinzón claimed he saw land. He shouted to Columbus, asking

Martín Pinzón was eager to be the first to sight land and receive Queen Isabella's prize: 10,000 maravedis (about $700 in gold) each year for the rest of his life.

for the reward. Columbus fell to his knees and thanked God. The men climbed the rigging for a better view. They sang a hymn of thanks. Hopes ran high, for the land seemed to be less than 50 miles (80 kilometers) away.

Columbus "ordered the ships to leave their course, which was west, and for all of them to go southwest where the land had appeared." The sea was calm. They sailed on and on until night fell.

The next day they realized their mistake. Columbus wrote, "They recognized that what they had been saying was land was not land but sky." Disappointed, Columbus ordered his fleet to turn west again.

On they sailed. More birds. More seaweed. More driftwood. But no land. For three weeks, no land. Hope turned to fear. Then the steady winds carrying them west died down to soft breezes. With little wind, the ships barely moved. They just wallowed in the sea.

The men were unhappy. They had suffered

enough. What if they ran out of food? some grumbled. What if Columbus were mad? others argued. What if they could not find their way back home? a few muttered.

Then, at sunrise on October 7, the cry *"Tierra! Tierra!"* was heard from the *Niña*. The crew raised a flag and fired a cannon. Land at last!

By sunset everyone knew the "land" was only another cloud. No land in sight.

By Columbus's measuring, they should be very near the Indies. The men did not care. If land was not found in three more days, they would throw Columbus overboard. They would return home without him.

Three more days, Columbus agreed, then he would order his ships to sail east to home. Little did he know that he was less than 200 miles (322 kilometers) from land.

The winds picked up. The three ships made good speed. The sailors saw more signs of nearby land. The *Niña* picked up a green branch with a flower on it.

The *Pinta* picked up a "little stick fashioned, as it appeared, with iron." Columbus wrote, "With these signs everyone breathed more easily and cheered up."

Once again all eyes searched for land. Everyone, including Columbus, wanted the reward offered by Queen Isabella. All wanted the silk jacket Columbus promised.

At ten o'clock on the night of October 11, Columbus claimed to see land. But he was not sure. "I saw a light, although it was so faint I did not wish to affirm it was land...I saw it once or twice and it was like a small wax candle that rose and lifted up." Thus Columbus himself claimed to be the very first to see land. And he claimed Queen Isabella's prize.

Two hours after midnight Pedro Gutierrez shouted, "*Tierra! Tierra!*" This time he was right.

In the morning they "reached an islet which was called Guanahani in the language of the Indians."

Columbus thought he had reached the Indies.

A NEW WORLD

I MAGINE THE EXCITEMENT ABOARD THE ships that night. This time there was no doubt. They had reached land.

What land, they did not know. But that day, October 12, 1492, they would find out.

At sunrise, Columbus searched for a safe place to anchor. Warm breezes carried wonderful smells to the ships. The men aboard gazed hungrily at the green of the trees. However, huge waves crashing on the reefs kept the excited sailors from landing.

At last a lookout spotted a break in the reef. Flags were raised. Colorful shields were hung from the railings. Columbus put on a scarlet jacket. His officers dressed in their best. Sailors armed themselves with lances, swords, and crossbows. Boats were lowered.

"I went ashore in an armed launch," Columbus wrote. The beach was long. The water was shallow. They rowed as close as they could. Then Columbus and the two Pinzón brothers waded ashore.

Columbus went first. He carried a royal banner. The Pinzóns held flags bearing a green cross and the initials of Isabella and Ferdinand. All three mariners had tears in their eyes.

Columbus lowered his flag. He fell to his knees and kissed the ground. The others did the same.

Columbus stood. He called to his men to witness his taking possession of the land. Even though the island was populated, he claimed it for the king and queen. He called it "San Salvador," the island of the Savior.

The natives of San Salvador watched from the safety of the forest. Imagine their thoughts as they watched these strange men come onto their island.

Columbus landed on the island of San Salvador on October 12, 1492. Natives of the island called it Guanahani, which means iguana.

"We saw naked people," Columbus wrote. "In order that they would be friendly to us...I gave them red caps, and glass beads and many other things of small value." Columbus was delighted with their response. "They took so much pleasure and became so much our friends that it was a marvel."

Columbus did not want to fight these "Indians," as he called them. He wanted to learn if they had gold. He wanted them to follow the Catholic religion. "I recognized that they were people who would be better converted to our Holy Faith by love than by force."

Columbus had met the gentle Taíno people, the inhabitants of Guanahani. The Taíno people lived on these scattered Caribbean islands. They were ruled by a chief called a *cacique*. Their families lived together in houses made from thatch, woven mats, and strong poles.

The Taíno people were skilled wood-carvers. They wove wonderful hammocks of cotton. These were the first hammocks ever seen by Europeans. Columbus took hammocks back with him.

The best guess is that 600 to 1,200 Taíno people lived on San Salvador in 1492. Columbus was impressed by their gentleness. Their trust struck him as well.

"They do not carry any arms nor are they acquainted with them. I showed them swords, and they took them by the edge and through ignorance cut themselves. They have no iron." Used to stone

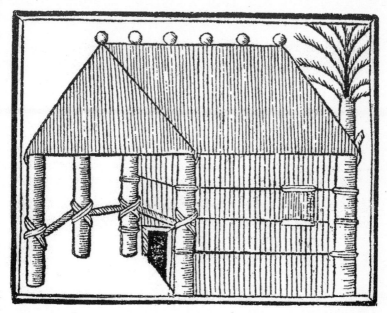

This drawing shows what a Taíno house may have looked like when Columbus landed.

and bone tools, the Taíno people did not understand the sharpness of steel.

The Taíno people were also very generous to Columbus and his men. "They took everything and gave of what they had very willingly." Some Taíno people swam out to the ships to trade. "They brought us parrots and cotton thread in balls and javelins and many other things. They traded them to us for other things which we gave them, such as small glass beads and bells."

Columbus had met his first "Indians." The Taíno people had met their first Europeans.

At sunrise on October 13, more Taíno people came to the beach. "All were young and of good stature, a very handsome people," Columbus wrote. "They came to the ships in dugouts made from the trunk of one tree, like a log boat. So big that in some of them 40 to 50 came. They row with a paddle like that of a baker and go marvelously." These were the first canoes Columbus had ever seen.

These Taíno people came to trade. More cotton, parrots, and javelins. Columbus, however, wanted something else: gold. He wrote, "I was attentive and labored to find out if there was any gold." The Taíno people had some.

"I saw that some of them wore a little piece hung in a hole they have in their noses." Columbus wanted to know where they had gotten the gold.

"By signs I was able to understand that, by

rounding the island to the south, there was a king who had large vessels of it and had very much gold."

Columbus decided to wait another day before searching for this wealthy king. "I will go to seek gold and precious stones," he wrote.

Columbus explored San Salvador. He was delighted by what he found. "This island is quite big and very flat and with very green trees and much water and a very big lake in the middle and without any mountains." He paused and added, "All of it so green that it is a pleasure to look at it."

But he found no gold other than what the natives wore. Columbus knew gold was nearby. After all, these were just small islands near the Indies. Somewhere close, he believed, lay China, Japan!

He had another idea to please the queen and king: slaves. Columbus was already aware of the gentleness of the Taíno people. "They would be good and intelligent servants," he wrote in his *diario*.

Believing the Taíno people had no god, Columbus wanted to save their souls. "I believe they would become Christians very easily, for it seemed to me that they had no religion."

He decided to take six Taíno people back to Spain. "At the time of my departure, I will take six of them from here to Your Highnesses in order that they may learn to speak [Spanish.]"

The men Columbus "took" helped him immediately. They told by signs of other islands nearby. They served as pilots to guide him. "And they named by their names more than one hundred."

Columbus would continue his search for the Indies. "I looked for the largest island."

On October 14, the ships set sail again. Columbus had first thought San Salvador was Japan. Now he knew better. No gold, no silks, no spices here.

But on the other islands? He would find out.

GOLD, MORE GOLD, AND DISASTER

COLUMBUS WAS NOT THE FIRST European to reach the Americas. But he was the first to return with proof of his adventure. Yet he was lost the whole time. Even after his fourth voyage to the New World, Columbus thought he had reached the Indies. He died thinking so.

Where had he first landed? Which island in the Caribbean is San Salvador? Even today the location of Columbus's actual landfall remains a mystery. The best guesses are Samana Cay or Watling Island in the Bahamas.

Columbus's trail becomes easier to follow once

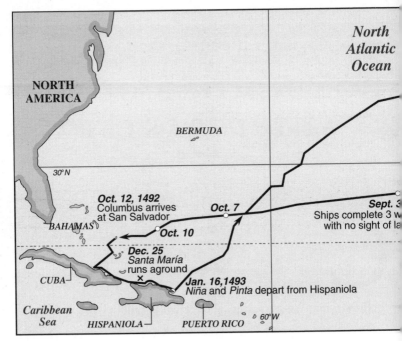

Columbus set out on his first voyage to the New World on August 3, 149

he left San Salvador. He believed he was among the many islands of the Indies. If the first island wasn't Japan, maybe the next island was. He began visiting island after island.

Such sailing was dangerous. The fleet had to dodge coral reefs. They had to avoid shallow waters. They had to be wary of storms, which could wreck

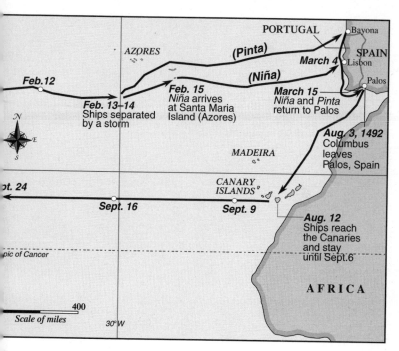

Map showing Columbus's route with the following labels:

PORTUGAL · Bayona · SPAIN · Lisbon · Palos · AZORES · MADEIRA · CANARY ISLANDS · AFRICA

Feb. 12

Feb. 13–14 Ships separated by a storm

Feb. 15 *Niña* arrives at Santa Maria Island (Azores)

(Pinta) · **March 4**

(Niña)

March 15 *Niña* and *Pinta* return to Palos

Aug. 3, 1492 Columbus leaves Palos, Spain

Aug. 12 Ships reach the Canaries and stay until Sept. 6

Sept. 24 · **Sept. 16** · **Sept. 9**

Tropic of Cancer

400 Scale of miles 30°W

...e did not return to Spain until March 4, 1493.

them. Twisting and turning, the three ships made their way among the islands of the Bahamas.

But exploring each island was frustrating for Columbus. The tiny amounts of gold he saw hinted to Columbus that the wealth of the Indies must be near. If only he could find it.

The "Indians" kept signing to Columbus that

there was gold if only he sailed south. Some told of a big island named Colba. Today we call it Cuba. To Columbus it sounded like Cipango. Japan!

"There I will speak with the King and see if I can get the gold that I hear he wears."

On October 28, Columbus reached Cuba. He found a small fishing village. But the people had fled when they saw his sails. He sent men inland to find the king. They carried letters from Queen Isabella and King Ferdinand.

The men found a village tucked away in the mountains. They met the local *cacique*. The "Indians" bowed and kissed the feet of the "men from the sky" as they called the Spaniards.

When asked about gold, the natives answered that there was none on the entire island. Disappointed, the men marched back to the shore. Along the way, they saw men and women smoking a burning herb that they called *tobacos*. This was the first time Europeans had ever encountered tobacco.

Columbus was as determined as ever to find gold.

So the fleet sailed on from island to island. One night, Martín Pinzón tired of such tactics. Without asking Columbus's permission, he ordered the *Pinta* to sail away.

This action made Columbus very angry. Was Pinzón trying to claim glory for himself? Was he going to fill the *Pinta* with gold and not share it? Or had the tiny *Pinta* been lost in a storm never to be seen again?

The *Santa María* and the *Niña* continued the search on their own. They landed on Bohío in early December. Columbus named it Hispaniola to honor Spain. Today Haiti and the Dominican Republic share this island. Columbus and his men traded with the "Indians," asked for gold, and took on fresh supplies. The Taíno people told Columbus they were ruled by the powerful chief Guacanagarí.

The chief, hearing of Columbus, sent him gifts. One was a mask with gold on it. Guacanagarí invited Columbus to his village. The chief sent more gifts. Columbus at first distrusted Guacanagarí. But the lure of gold was too strong. He sailed to meet the great chief.

The sea was very calm. The *Santa María* and the *Niña* cruised along the coast. It was Christmas Eve. The men celebrated. Tired, Columbus went to sleep. So did the crew of the *Santa María*. Against Columbus's orders, one of the ship's boys manned the steering tiller.

"I had forbidden this throughout the voyage. Regardless of wind, no boy should be entrusted with the tiller. But to tell the truth, I felt quite safe about the reefs and shoals." It was just after midnight, early Christmas day. Ever so gently, the *Santa María* hit a reef. No one, not even Columbus, awoke.

"When the boy felt the rudder run aground and heard the noise, he cried out. I heard him and got up immediately, and understood what had happened before anyone else."

Columbus ordered some sailors into a small boat. They were to pull the *Santa María* off the reef. Much to Columbus's horror, they fled to the *Niña*.

"The water became even shallower [the tide was going out]; the ship would not move and then she began to list [lean]. Her seams opened, and the water began to come in." The *Niña* sent men to help. The *Santa María* kept sinking.

"I saw no chance of saving my ship, and to spare the lives of my crew I left her and went with them to the *Niña*."

Columbus wept. Was this to be the end of his voyage? The *Santa María* was sinking. The *Pinta* was gone. Only the little *Niña* was left. His dream of glory was now a nightmare of disaster.

Columbus sent word to Chief Guacanagarí. "When the King heard of our misfortune, he wept and at once sent his people with many large canoes to the ship. So, we all began to unload together, and it was not long before we had cleared the entire deck."

The *Santa María*'s supplies were carried to the island. The chief put guards around the goods. Columbus was very pleased, for he wrote, "I can

When the Santa María *began to sink, Chief Guacanagarí sent help.* *Columbus called him "virtuous above all."*

assure Your Highnesses that the goods would not have been better looked after in Castile [Spain], and that not so much as one shoelace was missing."

The chief signed to Columbus that he should cheer up. Despite his difficulties, Columbus did just that. He invited the chief to dine aboard the *Niña.* The chief treated Columbus to a feast of lobster and yams. Columbus promised to protect the chief and his people from the Caribs who were feared by the

Taíno people. (From Carib we get the word *Caribbean*). Columbus fired off muskets to show the Taíno people his power. They had never before seen or heard such weapons.

Columbus decided that the wreck of the *Santa María* on Christmas Day was a sign from God that he was meant to be there. The chief gave him gold rings, necklaces, and masks. The men traded for more gold. The Taíno people told Columbus of much more gold on the island.

Columbus decided to build a fort. He would leave men there. They would become friends of the "Indians." And they would look for more gold. Columbus promised to return as soon as possible.

This seemed to be a good idea. After all, the *Niña* could not carry everyone back to Spain. "Many of my people asked me to allow them to remain," Columbus wrote. Forty men were to stay behind to make the new colony.

Wood from the *Santa María* was used to build the fort. A moat was dug around the fort. The *Santa María*'s cannons were put in place to guard the fort.

To impress the "Indians," the *Niña*'s cannons were fired at the wreck of the *Santa María*.

Columbus called the fort La Navidad, which is Spanish for Christmas. He did this because his ship ran aground on Christmas morning.

The *Niña* was loaded with food and fresh water. She was preparing to return to Spain. Columbus did not want to leave. He had not finished exploring the islands. He had not gotten enough gold. He had not found the wealth of the Indies.

But he had only the *Niña* left. It was time to sail home.

HOMEWARD BOUND

THE SUN ROSE ON JANUARY 4, 1493. The *Niña* raised her sails. Columbus explored the north coast of Hispaniola for a while. Then he left. But he would return. It was a new year in the New World. He would be back.

Three days later, the lookout on the mast spotted a sail. It was the *Pinta*! She wasn't lost after all. Columbus was relieved. Now he had two ships. But he was angry with Captain Pinzón. He accused him of looking for gold on his own.

It was true. Pinzón had found gold, which he split with his men. He had taken six captives. Columbus freed them.

Together, the ships sailed along the coast for two weeks. On January 16 the wind picked up. It was blowing east, toward Spain and home. The sails were raised. The compass was checked. Columbus ordered the course set east. The *Niña* and *Pinta* began the journey back across the Atlantic Ocean, an ocean not as unknown as before.

The good winds held. The ships sped along. One day they sailed 274 miles (441 kilometers), the most ever. By early February, they thought they were close to the Azore Islands off the African coast.

Then the good weather changed to bad. The sea grew rougher than ever before. The winds blew stronger. Before long a terrible storm was upon them. The ships tossed and turned. Waves crashed over them. The men were wet and miserable.

The storm got worse. Flares were lit on both ships so they could see each other. Columbus did not want to lose the *Pinta* again. By morning, she was no longer in sight. The *Niña* was alone once more.

Day after day the storm continued. Every man took turns at the pumps. They desperately tried to keep the *Niña* from sinking. The sailors worried. They prayed to reach safety. Columbus worried. He prayed. Still the storm continued.

Columbus feared that if the ship sank, the news of his great venture would be lost. He decided to make a shortened copy of his *diario*. "I therefore wrote on parchment [paper], briefly as the situation demanded, about how I discovered these lands, as I had promised to do, and about the length of the journey and the course, about the excellence of the country and the customs of it people, and of how I had left Your Highnesses' subjects in command of everything I had discovered."

He wrote that a great reward would be given to whomever found his message and sent it to Queen Isabella. He wrapped the parchment in a piece of waxed cloth for protection. This was placed in a cake of wax and then sealed in a large wooden cask. "I secured it with hoops and cast it into the sea."

That cask carried his last hopes.

The storm raged for another day and night. Then the lookout called, "*Tierra!*" The Azores at last!

Columbus throws a copy of his diario into the ocean during a fierce storm.

These islands were owned by Portugal. It wasn't Spain. But they were almost home.

Columbus rested. He had been awake for three days and nights. His legs were so cold and wet he could barely walk.

The people of the Azores could scarcely believe Columbus's tale. No ships could have survived that storm! Columbus could not possibly have sailed from the Indies!

Half the crew went ashore to pray at a local church. The Portuguese made them prisoners. This angered Columbus. He threatened to destroy the island. The men were released.

The *Niña* was given fresh supplies of bread, meat, and water. On February 24, they set sail again. Spain was their goal.

But another huge storm roared upon them. Once again the tiny *Niña* was tossed and turned. She almost sank. Columbus and his men prayed and prayed. The sails were torn to ribbons.

Columbus wrote, "We went through so terrible a storm we thought we were lost for the seas went over the ship from both sides and the winds seemed to lift her into the air. Water from the sky, and lightning on all sides."

On March 4, at dawn, they saw mountains through the rain. It was Portugal! With only one sail left, the *Niña* limped into port.

Columbus sent King John a letter asking permission to fix the *Niña* in Portugal. He promised he would then leave. But Columbus could not help bragging to King John that he had indeed sailed west to the Indies.

King John permitted Columbus to repair the *Niña* in Portugal. The king invited Columbus to visit him, for he wanted to hear of Columbus's adventures firsthand. Columbus took the "Indian" slaves with him to the king's court.

King John set a bowl of beans before one "Indian." He asked him to place the beans to show the many islands Columbus said he had found. The "Indian" did as he was commanded. King John could not believe it. He knocked the beans to the floor.

He ordered another "Indian" to place the beans. He put out even more!

King John grew angry at himself for not helping Columbus. He beat his chest and cried out, "O man of little understanding! Why did you let such an enterprise fall from your hands?"

Columbus boasted that the king should have listened to him. This angered the king's men. They wanted to kill Columbus. Then he could not tell the Spanish king and queen of his success. King John would not agree to murder.

Columbus wrote to Queen Isabella and King Ferdinand. He told them of his success. They quickly responded, commanding, "Our Admiral of the Ocean Sea and Viceroy and Governor of the Islands Discovered in the Indies" to come to them immediately! And they wrote the words Columbus wished to hear: "Do not delay in your going back."

The *Niña* weighed anchor again. Three days later on March 15, 1493, with flags flying, she sailed into the port of Palos. The men fired a cannon salute to announce their homecoming.

They had been gone half a year. Some had expected never to return home to their families. But they had!

Everyone flocked to see the sailors. They marveled at the parrots. They stared at the "Indians." They were excited by the gold.

Almost unbelievably, the lost *Pinta* sailed in that very evening.

Columbus's first voyage to the New World ended on a most happy note. He had proven that he could reach land by sailing west. This persistent son of an Italian weaver had shown the way. Columbus's dream had come true.

CHAPTER 12

THE SECOND VOYAGE

QUEEN ISABELLA AND KING FERDINAND were in Barcelona. So once more Columbus set forth. This time on land. What a procession it was! The admiral was dressed in new clothes made especially for such an important person. He rode in front on a horse, followed by his officers. Six captured "Indians" marched behind.

Again crowds gathered everywhere to see the admiral and the wonders with him: gold, strange people and colorful, squawking parrots. They gaped at "many other things never before seen in Spain or heard of," Columbus wrote.

Barcelona was ready for Columbus. The streets were decorated as if for a festival. The queen and king greeted Columbus. "They rose to meet him, as for a great lord, and made him sit down at once," wrote Bartolomé de Las Casas. They saw the wonders he brought: the "Indians," cages of parrots, chests of cotton and spices, skins of large lizards, and barrels of unusual fish. They heard his marvelous tales of his adventures, of the best harbors in the world, of lush islands, of gentle people, of fantastic animals.

Then Columbus brought out the gold: gold masks, gold crowns, gold jewelry. He held up nuggets of solid gold and handfuls of gold dust.

Queen Isabella and King Ferdinand had tears of joy in their eyes. They praised God. They praised Columbus. They made him a nobleman. Columbus could now have his own coat of arms, which only nobles could have. On his coat of arms Columbus would proudly display: five anchors to represent himself as Admiral of the Ocean Sea, islands near a continent for his discoveries, and a golden castle

King Ferdinand and Queen Isabella were very pleased with the treasures Columbus brought to them upon his return to Spain.

and crowned lion as symbols of honor from the queen and king.

And the queen and king ordered Columbus to prepare to return to the lands he had found as fast as possible.

Columbus was ready for this moment. He wanted

In 1493, Columbus received this coat of arms and was given the noble title Don.

more ships and more men. He wanted priests to convert the "Indians." He wanted settlers to build colonies. The queen and king agreed.

The new fleet of seventeen ships gathered in Cádiz. Among them was Columbus's stalwart *Niña*.

Columbus had no trouble getting crews for his ships this time. Everyone wanted to go to this strange new world. Everyone wanted gold. Twelve hundred men (no women) signed on. Columbus's trusted brother Diego joined him this time.

Columbus named his new flagship the *Santa María* in honor of his first ship. The ships were loaded with tools, food, seeds to plant, sheep, pigs, and horses. Plans were made for the colony. Time would be spent growing crops for food and hunting for gold.

On September 25, 1493, the eager adventurers set sail. Columbus's second voyage was underway.

Again, the first stop was the Canary Islands for fresh supplies. On October 13, exactly one year and one day after he made landfall in the New World, Columbus left the Old World of Europe behind.

Columbus set the western course. Good winds pushed the ships along quickly. Gone were the fears of the first voyage. The rolling Atlantic was no longer unknown. Columbus knew the way. In three weeks, they crossed the ocean.

Once more Columbus explored. He found more good harbors. He tasted pineapple for the first time. He and his crew looked for gold. They met more Native Americans. And they had their first fight with them.

Columbus sent men ashore to get fresh water. On their return, the men met a Carib canoe with four men, two women, and a boy aboard. The Caribs, hoping to escape, shot arrows at the Spaniards. One Spaniard was wounded. Another was killed. The Spaniards captured the "Indians" and took them to their ships.

Columbus sailed past Puerto Rico, stopping only for water. He wanted to reach La Navidad, the colony he had left on Hispaniola the January before. There would surely be casks and barrels overflowing with gold.

Columbus fired a cannon as he approached La Navidad. The fort did not answer. Flares were sent up. No answer from the fort.

Columbus went ashore. The fort and the houses were in ashes. All the Spaniards were dead.

What happened? Columbus wondered. Had the gentle Taíno people killed his men?

From Chief Guacanagarí and other Taíno people he learned the truth. Soon after the *Niña* had sailed, the men left behind began fighting amongst themselves. No one wanted to work on the fort. No one wanted to gather food. Everyone wanted gold.

The men attacked Chief Guacanagarí's villages. They took all the gold they could find. They forced the Taíno people to hunt for more gold. Then they moved inland. They attacked the villages of Chief Caonabo. His men fought back.

Then the Taíno people attacked the fort. They killed all the Spaniards there. The rest of Columbus's men fled into the forests. The Taíno people tracked them down and killed them. Soon no Spaniards were left alive.

Columbus had ordered the men of the colony to bury all the gold they found. Now he ordered his new men to dig in the fort to find the buried gold. They found only garbage.

The dead men were given a funeral. Columbus

This artwork was created in 1494. It shows the colony of Isabela, sometimes spelled Isabella.

would not give up. He was going to establish a colony on Hispaniola. Further east along the coast he built a town. He called it "Isabela" to honor the queen. He believed gold mines were nearby.

The Spaniards found a little gold. But hundreds got sick. It was too hot and damp. There were too many bugs. There was too much hard work.

Columbus would not give up. He sent twelve ships back to Spain to get more men and supplies. And he wanted 100 miners to dig for gold.

The men at Isabela began dying. The survivors wanted to leave. They turned against Columbus. To avoid conflict himself, Columbus gave command of

Isabela to his brother Diego. Columbus would continue looking for the "mainland of the Indies."

He was gone five months and did not find the Indies. He found more islands and only a little gold. Due to the weather and to stress, Columbus was frequently sick. He landed on the island of Jamaica but found nothing of interest.

Columbus returned to Isabela to find things worse, not better. His brother Barthlomew had come from Spain with three ships. He explained to Columbus that some of the unhappy colonists had rebelled, captured his three ships, and sailed home to Spain. The only good news was that Columbus's sons, Diego and Ferdinand, were now pages for Queen Isabella.

Before long, however, other ships came from Spain. The outlook improved. There was medicine for the sick men. There was food. There were healthy men to fight, search for gold, and build the colony.

Columbus built three new forts for protection. He

sent his men out to force the Native Americans to dig for gold. Those who refused were killed or enslaved. If they did not bring in enough gold, they were punished.

Many Taíno people fled to the mountains for safety. The Spaniards hunted them with hounds. Thousands died from disease or starvation. The coming of the Spaniards to Hispaniola brought greed, conquest, and death.

Queen Isabella and King Ferdinand were becoming unhappy with Columbus. Columbus had jealous enemies at the royal court. Where was the gold he had promised? they asked. Where were the spices, jewels, and silks of the Indies? Why was he unable to govern his colony?

Frustrated with Columbus's lack of success, the queen and king sent Juan Aguado to the Isabela colony to investigate.

With his honor to defend and wealth to protect, Columbus knew he had to return to Spain. Once again aboard the *Niña*, he sailed home. It was March 1496. Columbus's luck was running out.

This time the *Niña* took three months to reach Spain. Columbus's homecoming was dismal. He could not see the king and queen for a month. They greeted him, but not with the same warmth as the first time.

In the meantime, Juan Aguado's report had damaged Columbus's reputation. The success of Columbus's first voyage had made many other men envious. They spread harmful rumors and lies about Columbus.

Columbus would not give up. He would not give in. He proposed a third voyage with only eight ships. Reluctantly, the queen and king agreed. They would send Columbus again, if only to head off the Portuguese.

But the monarchs did not rush into this new venture. Two years passed before the next fleet was ready. In May 1498, Columbus sailed on his third voyage to the Indies.

Aboard one of the ships was seventeen-year-old Bartolomé de Las Casas. Later, he copied Columbus's original journal, thus saving it before it was lost. De Las Casas became the first Catholic priest ordained in the New World. He also was the first European to speak out against how the Spanish ill-treated the "Indians." But this lay in the future. For the moment de Las Casas was excited to be sailing with Columbus.

CHAPTER 13

THE THIRD
VOYAGE: HOME
IN DISGRACE

COLUMBUS'S THIRD VOYAGE IS CALLED "the Southern Voyage." He had heard rumors that a great land lay opposite Africa. If he sailed south closer to the equator, he thought he would find this new land.

Three ships in the fleet went ahead to bring supplies to Santo Domingo. This town had been established by Bartholomew Columbus on Hispaniola. The other ships stayed with Columbus to explore. One was the plucky *Niña*. She had been rebuilt: new deck, new sails, new planking. She was loaded with supplies: flour, wheat, olive oil, cheese, and barrels of salt pork. Sometime in 1499, the *Niña* was sold. She then disappears from history's pages. She was the only one of Columbus's ships to make three voyages to the New World.

Trouble came immediately. By sailing south, Columbus entered the doldrums. Here no winds blow for days on end. Columbus's fleet drifted under the scorching sun.

"There the wind failed me and I came into so great heat and so intense that I believed the ships and people would be burned." Water barrels burst their hoops. The bacon and salt pork began roasting and rotting. It was so hot and evil-smelling below deck that no sailors dared venture there. "This heat lasted eight days."

Finally, a favorable wind blew up. "I steered westward, but I did not dare to go lower down to the south. I did not find a change in the temperature."

Two months into the voyage, Columbus saw three mountaintops. He called the island Trinidad. Never before had he sailed so far south. "There were houses

During a trip to Rome after the second voyage, the Niña *was boarded by pirates. She was eventually recovered.*

and very fair lands, as lovely and green as the orchards of Valencia, Spain, in March."

This had to be China, Columbus thought. Finally, his dream would come true.

But when he landed, Columbus found more Native Americans. Wanting gold, he showed them bowls of polished copper and other shiny things.

They did not understand. To impress them, Columbus ordered the ships' boys to dance. The drummer beat his drum.

The Native Americans were frightened by this display. "As soon as they observed the playing and dancing, they all dropped their oars and laid their hands on their bows and strung them, and each one took up his shield, and they began to shoot arrows."

Columbus sailed on. He glimpsed more mountains. He landed on what is Venezuela today. For the first time since the Vikings had done so, Europeans had stepped on an American continent. "I am of the belief that this is a great continent, of which nothing has been known until this day," Columbus wrote.

He did not risk taking more time to explore, for Columbus knew he was needed in Santo Domingo. After all, he was governor. He had to check up on his colony. His brother Diego was in command while he was gone. How did the colony fare? Had they found more gold?

Besides, he was sick with malaria. His eyes gave

him trouble. Exhausted from his labors, Columbus needed a rest. Reluctantly, he turned north to Santo Domingo.

What he found was a disaster. Santo Domingo was in rebellion. "I found almost half the people in revolt. They have made war on me to this day. At the same time there has been a serious conflict with the Indians."

Two hundred unhappy colonists had returned to Spain. With them they carried complaints about the Columbus brothers. Another 100 rebels had fled Santo Domingo. They lived in the mountains. They hunted for gold. They attacked the Native American villages.

Columbus offered to pardon these rebels. He would give them ships to return home. He would pay them their wages. It hurt Columbus to give in, but he had to. The rebels agreed to his terms.

Columbus wrote a long letter to Queen Isabella. He explained what had happened. He defended himself and his brothers. He sealed the letter and sent it to Spain with the rebels.

Christopher Columbus was a great sailor. He could find his way over the waves with no difficulty. He could command a ship or a fleet of ships with few problems. But on land his skills deserted him. He did not seem to be able to run a colony successfully. Neither could his brothers.

Not all of the problems were caused by Columbus. Many of the men who came to the New World were Spanish gentlemen. They came believing gold lay on the ground just waiting to be picked up. They did not want to hunt and dig for it. They did not want to dirty their hands by planting crops for food. They thought themselves above such work. So they forced the Native Americans to be their slaves and treated them harshly.

More Taíno people were killed. More died from hunger and disease. The Taino people fought back, but had little chance against the firepower of the Spaniards.

To complete the calamity, the Spanish gentlemen resented Columbus. He was Italian, not Spanish, they complained. He was a foreigner and an enemy of Spain. They grumbled that the brothers ruled the colony too harshly.

These complaints reached Queen Isabella and King Ferdinand. By now, Columbus had even more envious enemies in Spain. These men told lies about him. They said he was cheating the queen and king. They accused him of spying for Portugal.

The monarchs were growing tired of the difficulties created by Columbus. During the second voyage, the queen and king had sent an investigator to the New World. They would do so again.

This time they sent Francisco de Bobadilla, a trusted royal officer. He seemed to be a fair gentleman. He would find out what lay at the bottom of the complaints about Columbus and the colony.

Bobadilla reached Santo Domingo in 1500. Christopher and Bartholomew were away exploring. As Bobadilla sailed into the harbor, he saw men hanging from gallows. He was told Diego had ordered five more rebels to be hanged the following day.

Outraged at Diego's behavior, Bobadilla had Diego arrested and placed in chains. He then took all of Columbus's belongings, his home, his papers, and his maps. Bobadilla, eager for gold himself, would be the sole governor of Santo Domingo.

When Columbus returned, Bobadilla commanded that he be arrested and placed in chains. Bobadilla claimed the queen had ordered him to shackle Columbus.

But no one dared touch their Lord Admiral. Finally, a cook stepped forward. He placed iron chains on Columbus's wrists and ankles.

"I could not think why I was a prisoner," Columbus wrote.

Bartholomew was also shackled. Bobadilla immediately sent the three Columbus brothers to Spain.

Once at sea, the captain of the ship offered to remove Columbus's chains. Columbus refused. "I have been placed in chains by order of the

When Francisco de Bobadilla arrested Columbus, there was only one person willing to place him in chains.

Sovereigns and I shall wear them until the Sovereigns should order them removed."

Thus shamed, Columbus sailed home in his chains.

When he reached Spain, the queen and king were too busy to see him. Still in chains, Columbus went to a monastery. There he dressed as a priest. He wrote letter after letter to the queen. He begged to be allowed to come to court. He wanted to clear his name. Is this the way to treat the man who discovered "more land than all of Africa and

Europe"? Should the Admiral of the Ocean Sea, who found "more than seventeen hundred islands" for Their Majesties, be in chains?

Queen Isabella ordered his release. Columbus kept his chains for the rest of his life. He asked that they be buried with him.

Bartholomew and Diego were also freed. The three brothers were given money to buy clothes to appear at the royal court. On December 17, 1500, they bowed before their sovereigns. Columbus presented his case. The queen relented and restored most of his rights.

Columbus asked to be able to return once more to the New World.

The queen and king told him to await their decision. He returned to the monastery.

By now Columbus no longer had red hair. Over the years, his hair had turned white. He was fifty years old and ill. Disappointed, Columbus continued to write letters. He wrote to Queen Isabella. He wrote to the Pope. He wrote to anyone who might help him with his plans. He refused to give up hope.

His pleading worked. In May 1502, Columbus set sail again. Maybe the queen and king were tired of his complaints. Maybe they wished to keep other countries out of their new territories. Maybe they hoped Columbus would at last really reach the Indies. Whatever the reason, they gave him permission for a fourth voyage.

THE FOURTH AND FINAL VOYAGE

THIS WAS COLUMBUS'S LAST CHANCE. He would take only four ships. He would find the passage between the islands that led to the true Indies. He was no longer governor. He was forbidden to enter Santo Domingo. But he was still Admiral and Viceroy. His thirteen-year-old son, Ferdinand, sailed with him. His brother Bartholomew was aboard another ship.

The ships Columbus found were old. Their bottoms had been chewed by shipworms. The ships were leaking before he even left Spain.

On May 9, 1502, the small fleet headed out. "I had ships, crews, and supplies and my course lay to the island of Jamaica." He had been there once before but had not had time to explore or look for gold.

Columbus called this "the High Voyage." It proved to be the longest of his voyages. It was also the most dangerous and disappointing. But he did not know this when he left Spain one more time. Although he was sick, he remained determined to complete the voyage.

In 1502, Spain was not the only country with ships at sea. John Cabot of England had landed in New England. Vasco da Gama of Portugal had sailed around Africa and reached the true Indies. Vicente Pinzón of Portugal, the captain of the *Niña* on the first voyage, had returned to explore the New World on his own. He landed in what is now Brazil. Maybe this was Columbus's last chance to prove he could reach the real Indies by sailing west.

Columbus decided to follow the route of his second voyage. That ocean crossing had been quick and uneventful. He chose correctly and crossed in twenty-one days.

Columbus had been warned not to enter Santo

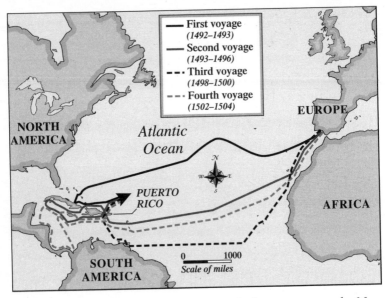

Between 1492 and 1504, Columbus made four voyages to the New World.

Domingo. "I was ordered not to come or go on shore."

How could he not look in on his struggling colony? He anchored just offshore. But from there he could see how his efforts were paying off. The huts from before were being replaced by impressive wooden buildings. The stone foundations of buildings still standing today were being laid.

Columbus also turned an eye to the sky. Trouble

was brewing. Already alert to the changing weather of the Caribbean, Columbus felt a hurricane coming. Signs of it were everywhere: The air felt heavy, the sky seemed on fire at sunset, dolphins and fish played at the sea's surface. The tides were higher than normal and the waves were long and smooth.

Columbus had to warn the people of Santo Domingo of the danger. He sent word to Commander Ovando who had replaced Columbus as governor.

Ovando read the message to his men. They laughed. What made Columbus think he could tell what God's weather would be? Besides, Ovando had other things on his mind. He was preparing thirty ships to return to Spain. The ships were loaded with gold. Some of the gold belonged to Columbus. Was this a trick by Columbus to get his gold?

Columbus sailed to the safety of another harbor nearby. His warnings proved true. Two days after the gold-laden ships sailed, the hurricane hit. Twenty-five ships and their crews were lost. Some of the ships' gold may still lie on the ocean floor. Four damaged ships limped back to Santo Domingo. Only one ship made it to Spain, the one with Columbus's gold!

Columbus suffered little damage. He lost a small boat and some anchors. No one died. "Although amazingly tossed about, Our Lord saved us, so that our ship suffered no damage at all."

Columbus continued to seek the passage to the true Indies. He sailed along the coast of Central America. For the rest of the year, Columbus searched for a route to the Indies. He and his men fought fierce mosquitoes and battled more storms. Columbus said one storm lasted eighty-eight days. He wrote, "I was never without . . . wind, water, and cloudbursts . . . so that the end of the world seemed to have come."

His ships suffered terribly. "The seams of my vessels opened, the sails tore, and I lost anchors, stays, and cables."

Ferdinand agonized with the others on the ship. He wrote, "With the heat and the wetness, the biscuit became so verminous that, God help me, many awaited the coming of night to eat so as to not see the maggots in it."

Another storm blasted them. Columbus wrote, "When I thought it was finished, it was only beginning. The seas boiled like a cauldron on a great fire. The crews were so bruised and beaten that they wished for death."

The men wished to quit. They wanted to go home. Enough was enough. "No!" exclaimed Columbus.

Days turned into weeks. Weeks turned into months. Still no passage. They landed in Honduras, Nicaragua, and Costa Rica. They landed in Panama. No one knew that the Pacific Ocean lay 30 miles (48 kilometers) away. Nine years would pass before Vasco Nuñez de Balboa gazed upon the Pacific after crossing Panama on foot.

Soon 1502 became 1503. Still Columbus searched. He was sick with malaria. The men were exhausted. One ship was in such bad shape it was abandoned. The others were riddled with holes from the shipworms. The men pumped out the water.

As they sailed south, Columbus and his crew faced a fierce storm during the fourth voyage.

They used pots and pans to empty the water. A second ship was abandoned.

Columbus worried about his men and ships. He also worried about his young son, Ferdinand. Despite Columbus's worries, Ferdinand was strong and cheered up the sailors. "The distress of my son Ferdinand, whom I had there, racked my soul, the more since I saw him, at the tender age of thirteen years so exhausted and for so long a time. Our Lord gave him such courage that he revived the spirits of the others, and he acted as if he had been a sailor for eighty years."

Columbus grew seriously ill. Ferdinand helped him. "He consoled me. I had fallen ill and had many times come to the point of death," Columbus wrote.

The men were defeated. Columbus ordered the two ships that were left to sail to Santo Domingo. There the men could rest and the ships be repaired.

Another violent storm struck. The ships, already weakened, were sinking. They stayed afloat until they reached Jamaica in June 1503. To save the ships from sinking, Columbus ordered them run aground.

They were marooned on Jamaica. Their food was almost gone. What was left was spoiled. They were over 100 miles (161 kilometers) from Hispaniola. No one knew where they were. No Spanish ships came to Jamaica, for Columbus had found no gold there on his first visit.

Diego Mendez, a loyal officer, traded a brass helmet, a coat, and one of Columbus's best shirts to the Taíno people for a canoe. Mendez would sail to Santo Domingo for help. But he was captured by hostile "Indians." Somehow, Mendez escaped and returned to Columbus.

Mendez tried again. Joined by another officer, he sailed the 400 miles (644 kilometers) to Santo Domingo. There, he chartered a boat and returned to Columbus. Mendez had been gone eleven months.

While he was getting help, the Spaniards on Jamaica quarreled among themselves. Forty-eight rebelled and tried to flee Columbus's command. They failed.

At one time Columbus and his men were starving. The "Indians" had at first traded food to them. Now they refused, for the Spaniards ate so much. "We consumed more in a day than they ate in twenty, and their demand for our truck [trade] fell off." The "Indians" did not want any more glass beads, brass bells, or rings.

Columbus, knowing an eclipse of the moon would happen on February 29, tricked the Native Americans. The eclipse meant that the moon would seem to slowly disappear and then gradually reappear.

Columbus told the Taíno people that they must give him more food. If they refused, he would make the moon disappear, forever. He made them promise to treat the Spaniards well. If the Taíno people did these things, Columbus promised the moon would return.

As the eclipse began, Columbus pretended to make the moon disappear. The Taíno people agreed to what Columbus asked. He pretended to order the moon back as it reappeared.

When help finally arrived in June 1504, only 100 out of 140 men and boys had survived. The rescued men were taken back to Santo Domingo. There, Columbus chartered a ship for Spain.

Columbus tricked the Taíno people into believing he could control the moon. From that time on, they gave the explorers the food they needed.

On September 12, 1504, Columbus sailed from the New World for the last time. Having failed to reach the Indies, Columbus returned to Spain in November a defeated man. Although he had wealth now, he was sick and aged. Columbus, Admiral of the Ocean Sea, was not even called to see the queen, for she lay dying.

After Queen Isabella died, Columbus followed King Ferdinand as the royal court moved around

Spain. He begged for his titles to be fully restored. King Ferdinand gave him gold instead. But Columbus felt he was entitled to more. The king, tired of Columbus, ignored him.

Columbus finally settled in a small home in Valladolid, Spain. He grew sicker and took to bed. There he ranted and raved. He believed he was a failure. Next to his bed, he kept his hated chains and a box of gold from the New World.

On May 20, 1506, Christopher Columbus died. His sons, Diego and Ferdinand, were with him. His brother Diego and two loyal shipmates were there, too. No one from the royal court bothered to come.

As Ferdinand later wrote, "Suffering greatly from the sorrow of finding himself fallen from his high estate, he gave up his soul."

No one knows exactly where Columbus is buried. Some claim it is in Valladolid. Others say he was buried on Hispaniola or Cuba.

Ferdinand wrote perhaps the best epitaph for his father. One of Columbus's favorite books was Seneca's *Medea*. In it Seneca predicts, "An age will

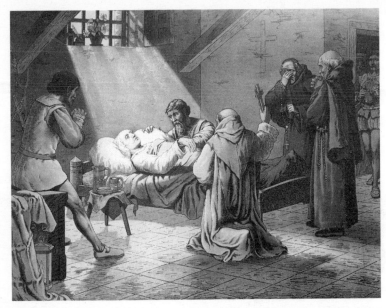

A small group of people gathered around Columbus during his final days. Christopher Columbus died on May 20, 1506, in Valladolid, Spain.

come after many years when the Ocean will loose the chains of things, and a huge land lie revealed."

With a quill pen and ink Ferdinand wrote next to Seneca's words, "This prophecy was fulfilled by my father...in the year 1492."

THE IMPACT OF COLUMBUS

COLUMBUS CHANGED THE COURSE of the world. This determined son of a weaver had a dream. He set forth to realize his dream. By doing so, he brought the Old World and the New World together in a lasting relationship. His landing in that New World is remembered in the United States on Columbus Day every October 12.

There is no doubt that Columbus was a master mariner. He proved one could safely cross the Atlantic Ocean. Although he died thinking he had indeed reached the Indies, we know he did not.

Columbus has had many places named in

his honor. The country of Colombia and Washington, District of Columbia, are named for Columbus. Mountains, lakes, and the Columbia River are named for him. Thirty states have cities and towns named after Columbus. A space shuttle is called *Columbia*. Throughout Central America, South America, and the Caribbean places bear Columbus's name.

Why isn't America named in his honor? Why is it called America instead of Columbia? It is a curious story.

Amerigo Vespucci of Florence sailed to the New World in 1499. He traveled with one of Columbus's rivals. He wrote a book about his travels to the New World. In it, he claimed to have discovered new lands. Another writer, having read Vespucci's claims, suggested that the new lands be named America in his honor. Published in 1507, this book used the word America for the first time ever. It was read widely throughout Europe. By the time the writer realized his mistake, it was too late. People were used to calling the New World "America" and America it remained.

This statue of Christopher Columbus was a gift from the citizens of Genoa, Italy, to the citizens of Columbus, Ohio. The statue was unveiled on October 12, 1955.

Columbus's encounter with the native peoples in the New World changed them forever. Many were killed or enslaved. Most lost their homelands. They died from European diseases against which they had no immunity. For many Native Americans, then and now, Columbus's coming is no reason to celebrate.

These first Americans also changed the world, for they sent many new things to the Old World. Potatoes, tomatoes, pumpkins, pineapples, turkeys, tobacco, chocolate, canoes, snowshoes, hammocks, and dozens of other things were new to Europe. Native Americans influenced the cooking and eating habits of millions of Europeans. Imagine spaghetti from Italy without tomato sauce!

And all that gold. Not only did Columbus return with gold, many other explorers brought back gold, too. This gold brought great wealth, especially to Spain. With her newfound riches, she became one of the most powerful countries in Europe.

The gold impacted the "Indians," too. To find it, they were forced to dig for it. Much of the gold they had was taken from them. Huge treasures of masks, jewelry, and other items were melted down. The gold was made into ingots and shipped to Spain. Rubies, emeralds, and other precious stones were taken, too.

In 1992, the five hundredth anniversary of Columbus's first voyage was remembered. His encounter with America was also mourned for the changes it brought to the world and to the Native Americans.

What if Columbus had not been so stubborn? What if he had not been so determined to follow his dream? What if he had given up and not persuaded Isabella and Ferdinand to support his "Enterprise of the Indies"?

Who would have been the first explorer to reach the Caribbean and South America if Columbus had failed?

These are questions history asks but cannot answer. For in 1492, Columbus did sail into the unknown and onto the pages of history.

CHRONOLOGY

1451   Christopher Columbus is born. His exact birthday is not known.

1466   Around this time, Columbus makes his first sea voyages.

1476   Columbus is shipwrecked. He moves to Lisbon, Portugal.

1476   Columbus sails the North Atlantic to England and Iceland.

1479   Columbus marries Dona Felipa de Moniz de Perestrello. They live in Lisbon, Portugal.

1480   Columbus's first son, Diego, is born.

1484   Dona Felipa dies.

1485   Columbus and Diego move to Spain.

1486   Columbus first tells the Spanish queen Isabella of his plan to sail west to reach the rich Indies.

1488   Ferdinand, Columbus's second son, is born. His mother is Beatriz Enríquez de Harana.

1492   (April 17) Queen Isabella and King Ferdinand agree to help sponsor Columbus's voyage.

1492   (August 3) The *Niña*, *Pinta*, and *Santa María* set sail from Palos, Spain.

1492   (October 12) Columbus lands on an island in the Caribbean.

1492   (December 25) The *Santa María* sinks off the island of Santo Domingo. Men are left behind to build a colony.

1493   (March 15) Columbus returns home to Spain aboard the *Niña*. The *Pinta* returns, too.

1493   (September 25) Columbus sails on his second voyage to the New World.

1496   Columbus returns from his second voyage.

1498   Columbus sails on his third voyage to the New World.

1500   Columbus returns from his third voyage.

1502   Columbus sets sail on his fourth and final voyage to the New World.

1504   Columbus returns from his fourth voyage.

1506   (May 20) Christopher Columbus dies in Valladolid, Spain.

1992   The five hundredth anniversary of Columbus's first voyage

BIBLIOGRAPHY

Primary Sources

Columbus, Christopher. *The Four Voyages of Columbus*, edited by Cecil Jane. New York: Dover, 1988.

Columbus, Christopher. *The Log of Christopher Columbus*, translated by Robert Fuson. Camden, Maine: International Marine Publishing, 1987.

de Las Casas, Fray Barthlomew. *The Diario of Christopher Columbus's First Voyage to America, 1492–1493,* transcribed by Oliver Dunn and James E. Kelley, Jr. Norman, Oklahoma: University of Oklahoma Press, 1989.

Secondary Sources

Asimov, Isaac. *Christopher Columbus*. Milwaukee: Gareth Stevens, 1991.

Levinson, Nancy. *Christopher Columbus: Voyager to the Unknown.* New York: Dutton, 1990.

Morison, Samuel Eliot. *Admiral of the Ocean Sea*. Boston: Little, Brown, 1942.

———, ed. *Journals and Other Documents in the Life Voyages of Christopher Columbus*. New York: Heritage Press, 1963.

Pelta, Kathy. *Discovering Christopher Columbus: How History Is Invented*. Minneapolis: Lerner, 1991.

Viola, Herman and Margolis, Carolyn. *Seeds of Change: Five Hundred Years Since Columbus*. Washington, D.C.: The Smithsonian Institution Press, 1991.

Weatherford, Jack. *Indian Givers: How the "Indians" of the Americas Transformed the World*. New York: Crown, 1988.

FURTHER READING

Conrad, Pam. *Pedro's Journal*. New York: Scholastic, 1991.

Dorris, Michael. *Morning Girl*. New York: Hyperion Books for Children, 1992.

Dorris, Michael. *Sees Behind Trees*. New York: Hyperion Books for Children, 1996.

Meltzer, Milton. *Columbus and the World Around Him*. New York: Watts, 1990.

Morison, Samuel Eliot. *Christopher Columbus: Mariner*. New York: Signet, 1984.

Osborne, Mary Pope. *Christopher Columbus, Admiral of the Ocean Sea*. New York: Dell, 1987.

Roop, Peter and Connie. *I, Columbus*. New York: Walker & Co., 1990.

Yolen, Jane. *Encounter*. New York: Harcourt Brace, 1992.

FOR MORE INFORMATION

The Columbus Navigation Homepage
This Web site, maintained by author and historian Keith Pickering, offers information on Columbus's navigation, ships, and crew. Includes a timeline and maps.
Web site: www1.minn.net/~keithp

The Columbus Santa María
Columbus, Ohio
The Columbus Santa María is a replica of Christopher Columbus's flagship. Visitors can tour the ship and discover what life was like for a fifteenth-century sailor.
(90 W. Broad St., Columbus, OH 43215-9019)
(614) 645-8760
Web site: www.santamaria.org

The Mariner's Museum
Newport News, Virginia
The Age of Exploration gallery includes information on Columbus, Portuguese exploration, the Vikings, and more. View maps and ship models or visit the hands-on Discovery Library to try using replicas of early navigation instruments.
(100 Museum Drive, Newport News, VA 23606)
(800) 581-7245
Web site: www.mariner.org/age/menu.html

PHOTO CREDITS

INDEX

Bold numbers refer to photographs